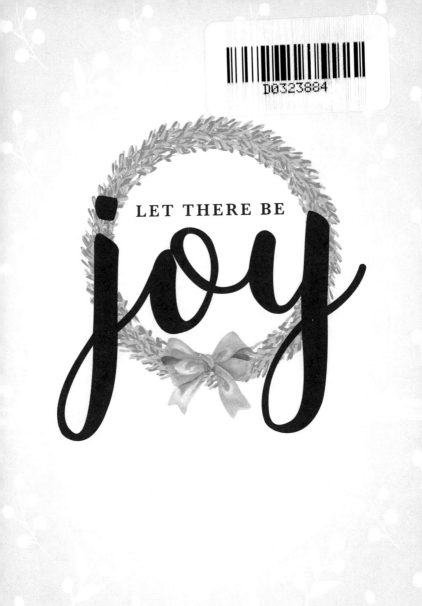

LET THERE BE

joy

LET THERE BE

joy

CAROL BURTON MCLEOD

BRIDGE LOGOS

Newberry, FL 32669

Bridge-Logos
Newberry, FL 32669

Let There Be Joy:
A Christmas Devotional
by Carol Burton McLeod

Printed in the United States of America.

International Standard Book Number: 978-161036-205-4

Library of Congress Control Number: 2017930922

Scripture quotations marked NASB are taken from the New American Standard Bible, Copyright 1960, 1962, 1963, 1968, 1971, 1972, 1973, 1975, 1977, 1995 by The Lockman Foundation. Used by permission.

VP 07-12-17

Dedication

Joyfully dedicated to my mom,

Joan Carol Boyce Burton Ormanoski,

Who makes every ordinary day seem like Christmas!

Endorsements

If I could pick a friend to walk with me through the Christmas journey, it would be Carol McLeod. Even though we live miles away from each other, through her new Christmas devotional I get this opportunity. You, too, can join Carol in preparing your hearts for Christmas, as you are not only encouraged by her faith, but also blessed by her giggles and illuminating joy.

— JANET LYNN MITCHELL, Author, Speaker

If ever there was an author who needed to do a devotional about Christmas, it is Carol McLeod. She loves Christmas, and when you get finished with this 25-day journey, you will too! You will not only love Christmas more, but you will understand why you love the season so much. And, it won't be a string of Christmas clichés you will take away. You will be enriched to the depths of your soul about the deepest meaning of the season, the special time each year when we celebrate the birthday of our King Jesus. Enjoy the trip through this brilliant devotional as you are hosted and guided by none other than Mrs. Christmas, Carol McLeod.

— CHRIS BUSCH, CEO LightQuest Media, Inc.

The joy of Jesus shines through Carol McLeod, so she's the perfect choice to write a devotional book about the joy of Christmas. Give Him a gift this Christmas as you use the insightful words from *Let There Be Joy* to draw closer to the One who truly is the reason for the season. I love this book!

— MICHELLE COX, speaker and bestselling author of
Just 18 Summers and the *God Glimpses* books

Carol's unusual candor and enthusiasm for God's Word shine through in her new Christmas devotional. She presents the familiar stories of Christ's birth in a new, refreshing way, reminding the reader of the joy of the season that might be smoldering in familiarity. Instead of the usual, Carol invites us to 'take a lingering and delicious look at the Christmas story.' I would highly recommend pouring some hot cocoa, grabbing a cookie right out of the oven, and snuggling into this sweet devotional. You will be blessed.

— DIANE KARCHNER, Ministry Director,
Renewing the Heart Ministries

Amidst the hustle and bustle of Christmas, I urge you to sit down by a crackling fire and bask in the warm glow of God's love for you. Carol's joyful and insightful daily readings usher you into the sweet simplicity of God's tender care demonstrated in the glorious gift of Christmas. In a season of busy-ness and expectation, give this gift to yourself: time at your Savior's feet in this beautiful devotional. You'll be glad you did!

— ERICA WIGGENHORN, Bible study author of
An Unexplainable Life and *The Unexplainable Church*

What I love about this devotional, is Carol's deep dive into the personalities surrounding the birth of our Savior and the insane intentionality that God orchestrated in fulfilling His promise to mankind. Carol brings to light ideas, meanings of names, and deep personal reflections on the Christmas story that will make your 25 days before Christmas more meaningful than they have been in years. We will read and reread this Christmas devotional for years to come!

— JOHNIE HAMPTON, CEO, Hampton Creative

Christmas is one of the hardest seasons of the year for many people. For this segment of women and men, singing, "Joy to the World" does not feel so joyful. They desperately need real encouragement, real strength, and real hope.

Let There Be Joy is the perfect tonic for the downtrodden, depressed, discouraged, or even those who are generally happy, but could use a fresh dose of new JOY. This easy to read devotional guide is not stuff and fluff -- it's a soul-boosting healing agent bubbling over with pure Christmas cheer.

— ANITA AGERS BROOKS, Common Trauma Expert,
International Speaker, and Award Winning
Author of Getting Through What You Can't Get Over

As you prepare to celebrate Christmas, join Carol McLeod on a unique journey, celebrating the birth of Christ. Experience the joy of the season, reading stories of people who walked by faith, believing God's promises, and praying with expectation and hope. Observe the power of praise, peace, and the presence of God revealed in the lives of people of faith. And discover the importance of asking the Lord to prepare your heart for this season of celebration. Don't miss this opportunity to embrace the joy of Immanuel, "God with us," with Carol McLeod in *Let There Be Joy!*

— KAREN JORDAN, Speaker and author of
Words That Change Everything

Christmas time is the most wonderful time of the year! But, it can also be one of the busiest and most chaotic. As a result, it's easy to lose your joy. Carol understands and has written a beautiful devotional that brings back the joy. Take a few minutes each day and journey with her to Bethlehem. You'll be delighted, inspired and revived as you celebrate the Savior.

— BECKY HARLING, International Speaker, Coach and the
Author of, *How to Listen So People Will Talk*

Table of Contents

Introduction

I love it all! I love everything about this miraculous, melodic, much-anticipated season of the year.

I love the cards that arrive daily flooding my mailbox with heartfelt greetings from friends and family from long ago and far away.

I love the calorie-laden goodies and the family recipes that have been passed down from generation to generation. I love knowing that when I make the fresh cranberry jello in preparation for Christmas dinner, that I am holding the same recipe card in my hands that my grandmother held in her hands over 50 years ago.

I love the smell of Christmas! My heart melts at the fragrance of the evergreen and peppermint and cinnamon that flood my home from the days before Thanksgiving right through to New Year's Day.

I love giving gifts to those I know the best and love the most. Even I, a woman who thinks that shopping is a waste of time, can't wait to hear the delight in my children's and grandchildren's voices on Christmas morning.

I love the childlike wonder that wraps itself around even the cynical world of entertainment.

I love the music ... oh! How I love the music of Christmas. Even now, I could weep thinking about the lyrics of the songs that are particular only to Christmas.

> "Mary, did you know that your Baby Boy has walked where angels trod? When you kiss your little Baby, you kissed the face of God!"

> "Immanuel! God is with us! And if God is with us, who could stand against us?! Our God is with us, Immanuel!"

> "I will hold you in the beginning, You will hold me in the end, every moment in the middle, make my heart Your Bethlehem, be born in me!"

> "Word of the Father, now in flesh appearing, O come let us adore Him, Christ the Lord!"

But what I love the most about Christmas is the story itself. I am breathless and humbled with the realization that, like Mary, I have been chosen to carry the Christ-child to my lonely world.

I am in awe and wonder, with the shepherds, that the joy of heaven would explode into the darkness of planet earth.

I am humbly joining in the worship with the Magi as I am invited to bow before the Infant King.

The first recorded words of God in the Bible are very familiar to most of us. *"Let there be light!"* was the declaration of the Creator God as He obliterated the darkness and void of the world pre-creation. His vibrant and powerful words washed away the dominion of darkness and He became the eternal Light of the world!

Thousands of years later, when Jesus came to restore what sin had stolen from creation, the angels made a declaration on behalf of the King of Heaven. Into the darkness of sin and shame, an angelic chorus heralded the news that delivered Jesus to earth, **"Behold, I bring you good news of great JOY which shall be to all the people; for unto you is born this day in the city of David, a Savior, who is Christ the Lord." – Luke 2:10**

When heaven announced the presence of Jesus into the battle-scarred world over Bethlehem, they sang, *"Let there be JOY!"*

My prayer for you this Christmas season is that you would rediscover the joy that belongs uniquely to Christmas. I pray that you would hear the song of the angels in your dark world and that you would join in the chorus that humanity has sung for hundreds of years. Don't allow the trappings of this time of year deny you of the dynamic and eternal song of Christmas.

A Savior has come and He has brought with Him heaven's joy!

Acknowledgements

Those whose voice is heard and whose presence is known in the Christmas story are a rich range of people, personalities and offerings. The shepherds, the angels, the wise men, a teen-age mother, a distraught fiance', a righteous and elderly couple were all part of the wonder that is known as "Christmas".

The folks who have helped me in my determination to write this book are much the same as those who showed up in the Christmas story. What an interesting yet dynamic group of people God has given me as a rare and glorious gift!

Thank you to my husband, Craig, who never complains about the lack of food, dearth of attention or absence of clean underwear in our home. Thanks for standing with me, honey, and for believing that I really am called to be a writer.

Thank you to the ones who have always embraced my enormous love for the Christmas season. I love you dearly, Matt and Emily, Chris and Liz, Jordan and Allie, Chris and Joy, and Joni. You turn every day into a holiday for me!

And then to the grandchildren who "get it"! They understand why Christmas is a reason for music, laughter and unmatched celebration. I love you so much Olivia, Wesley, Boyce, Elizabeth Joy, Amelia Grace, Jack and Ian. There is absolutely no one I would rather spend Christmas with than all of you!

Thank you to Craig's dear mother, Becky, aka Nanny, who loves each one of us with deep prayer and encouragement.

Thank you to my mother, Joan, and her wonderful husband, Leo, who have always stood with me in ministry and have continuously believed in the message of my heart.

Thank you to the staff at Just Joy! Ministries who are a delight to work with every day of the calendar year! I love you more than you know Monica Orzechowski, Angela Storm, Sarah Grice, Linda Zielinski, Terra Robinson, Joy and Chris Barker and Jordan McLeod.

Thank you to John Mason, my Literary Agent extraordinaire! Thank you for keeping all of the details in order and for going to bat for me time after time after time. There is no one like you, John! You are one in a million in my book!

Thank you to Suzi Wooldridge of Bridge-Logos who has opened the door for this book to be published. Your kindness is unmatched, dear Suzi.

And then, thank you to my friends who are among the greatest gifts I have ever been given. Shannon Maitre, Carolyn Hogan, Sue Hilchey, Kim Pickard-Dudley, Janie Sperrey, Lisa Keller, Christy Christopher, Jill Janus, Kim Schue, Dawn Frink, Marilyn Frebersyser, Lynn Fields, Patricia Apy, Camella Binkley and Suzanne Kuhn … I wouldn't trade you for the world!

Merry Christmas, everyone! I pray that you experience the joy of this miraculous season every day of every year of your life!

DAY 1

The Wonder of Righteousness

It's Christmas! The most wonderful time of the year! This season is miraculously wonderful not because of the scrumptious and sugary holiday cookies nor is it due to the lavish gifts found under the Christmas tree. Christmas is not defined by the reindeer who dance or by the shoppers who spend. Christmas is not "Christmas" because of decorations, or parties or even by the chestnuts that you might find roasting by an open fire.

Christmas is wonderful because of Him ... because of a Baby that was born long ago and yet continues to live on in the hearts and lives of millions who dare to declare, "Let there be joy!"

Will you join me on a journey to Bethlehem? Let's spend the next 25 days together and take a lingering and delicious look at the Christmas story found in the Bible. The historical account of the birth of Jesus didn't start in Bethlehem or even in Nazareth but it began with an elderly couple who knew the deep fulfillment of living wholeheartedly for God.

The Bible describes Elizabeth and Zacharias in the loveliest of ways: "They were both righteous in the sight of God, walking blamelessly in all the commandments and requirements of the Lord." — Luke 1:6.

Elizabeth and Zacharias had been married for many years and yet still had no babies. The heartache must have been wrenching for this man of prayer and his wife, but the Bible records they continued to walk blamelessly in every aspect of their relationship to the Lord.

For the priest Zacharias and for his faithful wife, Elizabeth, there had been no 3 a.m. feedings, no messy diapers and no sweet giggles and baby smiles. Their life had not turned out in the manner that they had hoped for or prayed for.

Disappointment is part of all of our lives, isn't it? Disappointment is surely part of the human experience.

How do you respond to disappointment? Do you use it as an excuse for over-indulgence or for griping and complaining?

Although Elizabeth and Zacharias had empty arms and dashed hopes, they continued to serve God wholeheartedly as the years continued to pass.

The Bible says that the prayer of the righteous one avails much! (James 5:16) When you continue to live a righteous life and continue to pray in spite of your human disappointment, your prayers will still get the job done!

The Bible also says that the righteous live by faith. (Hebrews 2:4) Elizabeth and Zacharias continued to walk by faith and not by sight.

Elizabeth's name actually means "God is my Oath". Elizabeth believed the promises of God long after others would have given up in frustration. She believed that God was listening to her prayers while her friends cooed over their own babies and then decades later when her circle of friends experienced the joy of rocking their grandchildren to sleep.

I hope that the first lesson you will learn in the Christmas story is to be patient with God. Trust God even when your circumstances are challenging and continue to live a righteous life through long days of disappointment. Pray fervently and believe that God is listening to your prayers. Continue to embrace a positive heart attitude even when you don't get your own way.

Allow the steadfastness of Elizabeth to remind you that true believers walk by faith and not by sight. Although she was barren, she continued to believe in the promises and in the nature of a faithful and miracle-working God.

BIBLE READING

- Luke 1:1-7
- James 5:16
- Hebrews 10:35-39

LET THERE BE JOY IN ME

For what are you praying this holiday season?

_____

_____

_____

What are some of the healthy responses or habits you can embrace while waiting for God to answer your prayers?

_____

_____

_____

DAY 2

Don't Give Up! Don't Ever Give Up!

Zacharias was chosen to be the priest this specific year who would enter the holy place in the Temple. It was his turn to offer incense to God on behalf of the people. However, as Zacharias was standing beside the altar of incense, he received a surprise visitor! The angel Gabriel had been sent from heaven to bring a life-changing message to the elderly Zacharias and Elizabeth.

"Do not be afraid, Zacharias, for your petition has been heard," were the words of the heavenly messenger at this history-changing moment. God had been silent for 400 years and at this very instant, Zacharias heard the audible answer for which he and his wife had been praying since the day of their marriage many, many years ago.

After all of the years of waiting and praying and believing, heaven's intervention was about to be experienced in the life and marriage of Elizabeth and Zacharias. Could it be true? Was it even possible after decades of marriage that they would conceive and bear a son? Would Elizabeth's elderly frame be able to withstand 9 months of pregnancy and then the pain of giving birth? I wonder if Zacharias' heart was joyously asking, "God, are You really this good?!"

It is true: God absolutely hears your prayers. He is listening intently to your requests and loves it when a believer comes to Him boldly and unashamedly. The Bible instructs Christians from every generation to ask and keep on asking, seek and keep right on seeking, knock and keep on knocking! (Matthew 7:7)

Don't give up, my friend, don't ever give up! The message of Christmas speaks into our silent world today: we serve a God Who answers the prayers of His children. While you wait, and while you pray, don't ever give up! Wait in faith and pray in hopeful expectation.

For what have you been praying? Perhaps you are praying for an unsaved spouse or for a rebellious child. Maybe your fervent prayer is for a breakthrough in finances or it might be that health concerns have dominated your prayers for years and years. You need to follow the example of Elizabeth and Zacharias and continue to pray with expectation and with hope!

It might seem like you haven't heard from God in 400 years but the answer and voice of God might only be one more prayer away.

Christmas is a time when we should all expect heaven's entrance into our dusty, dirty worlds. Christmas is a time that reminds us that miracles really do happen, that prayers are actually answered and that heaven is just one response away.

You honor God when you ask of Him the impossible! I believe that "Impossible" is what the God of Christmas does best!

BIBLE READING

- Luke 1:8-23
- Matthew 7:7-11

LET THERE BE JOY IN ME

What is the best answer to prayer that you have ever received?

_____

_____

_____

Make a list of others who are standing in faith for answers to their prayers. Pray for them today.

_____

_____

_____

DAY 3

Lord, Prepare Me for What You are Preparing for Me

In the days during which Elizabeth lived, it was not uncommon for pregnant women to go into seclusion when their pregnancies became visible. However, according to Scripture, Elizabeth, who was old enough to be a great-grandmother, apparently went into seclusion from the very first days of her unexpected pregnancy.

I have often wondered why Elizabeth chose to hide herself away much earlier than was culturally acceptable or required. I wonder if perhaps Elizabeth found it necessary to prepare her heart for God's plan. Elizabeth may have been so filled with thanksgiving and wonder that she knew preparing for motherhood was the single most important priority at her very advanced age.

I can picture tears coursing down her wrinkled and liver-spotted cheeks as she prayed, "Lord! A miracle! A bona fide miracle You have given to us!"

I wonder, as Elizabeth began the joy of making sweet little blankets and sewing precious garments of miniature clothing with gnarled and arthritic fingers, if her heart cried out to the God of the universe, *"Lord, prepare me for what You are preparing for me!"*

I believe that during these days of quiet, yet joyful contemplation, Elizabeth had a heart that was overflowing with gratitude. She may have been intent on changing her lifestyle during this time of delightful preparation in order to become the mother that raising a young man of greatness would require. Elizabeth was preparing her heart for the day of delivery and for the unexpected yet much anticipated blessing.

During this Christmas season, for what do you need to prepare your heart? Do you need to make some lifestyle changes in order to accommodate the destiny that God has chosen for you? For those that He calls to do a great work, He also calls away into His presence.

Christmas is the season of hope and miracles and it is also the season that calls all of us into a time of preparation for the destiny of God in our ordinary lives. I pray that you will take some time today, and every day during this wonderful season, to hide yourself in God's presence. Rather than wrap yourself in busy-ness and extravagance, snuggle up in His love for you and ask Him to reveal His destiny for your life.

I hope that you will pray with Elizabeth, and with me, *"Lord, prepare me for what You are preparing for me."*

BIBLE READING

- Luke 1:24 & 25
- Isaiah 40:28-30

LET THERE BE JOY IN ME

What is the great work that you have been called to partner in with God?

_____

_____

_____

What are some of the ways that you can prepare for the great work that God has called you to?

_____

_____

_____

What is your favorite Christmas Carol?

_____

_____

_____

DAY 4

Peace on the Battlefield of Life

British soldiers were spending Christmas Eve 1914 on a freezing, French battlefield during the intense fighting days of World War I. After four months of fighting, over a million men had perished in the bloody conflict. The bodies of dead soldiers were scattered between the trenches of the opposing armies.

Life in the trenches was despicable. Perpetual machine gun shelling took a high toll; the weather ushered in rain, snow and cold. The brave but lonely soldiers were never dry and never warm in these conditions. The flooded trenches in which the soldiers lived exposed the soldiers to trench foot and frostbite.

It was in the middle of a freezing battlefield in France, on December 24, 1914, that a miracle occurred! British troops watched in amazement as candle-lit trees appeared above the German trenches. The British troops raised a sign with the words, "Merry Christmas!" on it and the grandest holiday truce in all of recorded history began.

"From the German parapet, a rich baritone voice had begun to sing a song I remember my German nurse singing to me ... the grave and tender voice rose out of the frozen mist. It was all so strange ... like being in another world," a young British soldier wrote in his diary.

"Silent Night, Holy Night. All is calm. All is bright."

When the German soldiers finished singing, the British decided to retaliate. Rather than respond with the roar of a canon, these boyish army chaps from England sang,

"The first noel, the angels did say, was to certain poor shepherds in fields as they lay ..."

When the boys from jolly old England finished, *"Born is the King of Israel!"*, the enemy began clapping and struck up a rousing rendition of *"Oh Tannenbaum!"*

As the British troops began singing, *"Oh Come All Ye Faithful!"*, it was at that moment that the Germans immediately joined in. They were singing with the enemy.

This was a most extraordinary holiday event that was taking place in the middle of a blood-drenched battlefield! Two opposing nations were singing the same Christmas Carol in the middle of a fierce war. It is recorded that enemy soldiers then began to greet one another in the no man's land that just minutes earlier had been designated a killing zone. Soldiers joyfully wished one another, "*Merry Christmas*," and agreed not to fire their rifles on Christmas Day.

The good will spread down the entire length of the 27-mile British line. It has been told that German soldiers shared baked goods and cider with the British soldiers. A rousing soccer game began between the opposing nations while other soldiers just wanted to talk about Christmas at home.

Thousands of soldiers celebrated the birth of the Prince of Peace among the bodies of their dead.

A solitary voice began to sing "Silent Night" in French ... he was joined by another voice singing in German ... and finally the words were in English.

Who do you need to make peace with this season? Have you been engaged in a fierce battle that has extracted the very life from your soul? Christmas is a moment in history when peace is abundantly possible because of the Baby Who came to bring peace for all of the ages.

BIBLE READING

- Isaiah 53

LET THERE BE JOY IN ME

Is there someone that you need to forgive this Christmas season? Make a plan to reach out in love and then follow through. Perhaps you can meet for a cup of coffee, or send this person a Christmas note or a loving e-mail.

DAY 5

The Girl Next-Door

Mary had grown up in the same village as Joseph, a carpenter's son, who was several years older than she was. Perhaps they had admired one another from a distance ... perhaps Joseph had just been waiting for his darling Mary to grow up into young womanhood! When Mary was just 13 or 14 years old, it was settled between the two families. Mary was to become the wife of Joseph.

Engagement, or betrothal, at this moment in history held the commitment that marriage does today. Although Mary and Joseph were not living together and would stay pure until their wedding night, the only way out of a betrothal was divorce and the only reason that justified a divorce was adultery.

Mary was in her girlhood home one afternoon, maybe working

on her wedding attire, or sewing towels for her new home when she sensed someone in the room with her. Conceivably, Mary looked around to see if anyone had joined her.

"And coming in, Gabriel said to her, "Greetings, favored one!" The Lord is with you."

Christmas, for Mary, brought the challenge of understanding what the favor of God means in a person's life. Mary was about to learn that being highly favored by God does not mean a life of unbroken happiness nor does it promise that all of one's dreams will come true. There is actually a tremendous price to be paid by those who are highly favored by God. Favor means, simply, that God is willing to use an ordinary person for His greater plan.

God is willing to use the young, the uneducated and the inexperienced in His grand plan for humanity. Just as the favor of God targeted the womb of Mary, I believe that the favor of God is targeting everyone and anyone who is willing to be part of God's strategy at this historical juncture.

Christmas, for Mary, was about discovering the intimacy of the Lord's presence as never before. Mary was about to be confronted with the reality that favor happens when God places a piece of Himself into an earthly life. No longer was God a mere concept or a Divine Being Who never engaged Himself in the affairs of every day life. Because of Gabriel's message, the presence of God Himself had invaded the life of this young girl.

Experiencing the favor of God in new ways is one of the best parts of Christmas for me! To think that God would desire to use my ordinary life is a gift that I never imagined I could find under the Christmas tree of life!

Discovering a fresh lifestyle of intimacy in the presence of Jesus is God's life-changing Christmas gift to you this year.

Christmas proclaims to your world, "The Lord is with me ... and with you! What a wonderful surprise!"

BIBLE READING

- Luke 1:26-29
- II Chronicles 16:9
- Isaiah 9:2-7

LET THERE BE JOY IN ME

What difficult thing has the Lord asked you to do? Perhaps it is the favor of God that requires diligence in serving Him not only in easy assignments but especially in difficult ones.

_____

_____

_____

Spend some time today listening to Christmas hymns and Carols. Expect God to meet you during moments of worship.

_____

_____

_____

DAY 6

You Call This Favor?!

Mary was perplexed! A strange man had just entered her home and had started to talk about things like favor and God and greetings! Who was this assertive man and what in the world was he talking about?

I can nearly hear Mary's racing heartbeat as she attempted to process all that was happening around her this day. The Bible says, *"Mary was perplexed and wondered what kind of salutation this was"*. Mary's cheeks were probably flushed and her heart was beating wildly.

As the Angel Gabriel continued to tell the message of heaven to this young girl, perhaps Mary's fear subsided and a humble awakening began to dawn in her heart.

"The angel said to her, "Do not be afraid, Mary; for you have found favor with God." – Luke 1:30

Gabriel had heaven's perspective on this miraculous announcement and saw absolutely no reason for Mary to be afraid of what was about to happen.

Sweet Mary, who was trying to wrap her heart and mind around the message of the angel may have been incredulously pondering, *"Me?! God chose me?! I am the chosen one to carry God's child? I am to be the mother of the Messiah?"*

Christmas, for Mary, ushered in the understanding that God's ways are so much higher than human ways. Mary was learning, like all of us must, that when Divinity invades humanity ... Divinity always wins! Christmas is a reminder to me ... and to you ... and to Mary ... that His ways are always higher and better than anything that we could ever think of imagine.

Christmas has nothing to do with dancing elves, reindeer with red noses or snowmen who sing. Christmas is about an invasion! Christmas happens at the moment when heaven's light invades the darkness of planet earth!

Christmas will always drive the worst of sinners to ponder

what kind of salutation the Christmas story brings. Either Christmas is a bold-faced lie or it is ultimate truth. It can be nothing else.

Either the manger should be placed in the same category as elves, jolly old Saint Nicholas and flying reindeer ... or it is absolute, divine and eternal Truth.

Christmas is not about the holiday spirit that rushes toward us the day after Thanksgiving and compels us to shop, spend, and eat. Christmas is about the Holy Spirit bringing peace and joy through a Baby Boy to the mess that we have made of planet earth. It is about the power of heaven's reality invading one life. Christmas commences the moment when a person submits to the deep longing that has always existed to be overshadowed by all that He is and all that He does!

It happened for Mary ... and it can happen for you! Perhaps an appropriate prayer to pray this Christmas would be,

"Holy Spirit! Overshadow me! Overshadow my dreams, my preferences and opinions! Birth something new and something grand in me! Create something in me that will change this generation for the Kingdom of Christ!"

BIBLE READING

- Luke 1:29-35
- Psalm 17

LET THERE BE JOY IN ME

Finish this phrase: Christmas is …

_____

_____

_____

Perhaps you could make a list of 10 things that "Christmas is …" to you. Engage other people in this conversation with you this week!

_____

_____

_____

DAY 7

A Miraculous Interruption!

"For nothing will be impossible with God."

Luke 1:37

Christmas, for Mary, was learning the ultimate truth of this one statement: *"Nothing will be impossible with God!"*

When Christmas rolls around each year, we must embrace the absolute faith that nothing is impossible with God! Christmas is a reminder that we must always keep our focus on His Divinity and not on our frail humanity.

My friend, you honor God when you ask of Him the impossible. So this year, rather than giving Santa an enormous and materialistic list, perhaps it would be most sincere to change your focus from temporary to eternal, from material to priceless and then to ask God for your true heart's desire. Impossibility is God's specialty! It is what He does best! You serve a God Who loves to show Himself miraculous in the face of profound disappointment and darkness.

Most of us go through the Christmas season focused on self ... on what we want and desire and deserve. Some people want a new house ... or a great piece of jewelry ... or for all of our children to come home for the holidays. Some folks emphatically believe that they deserve a Christmas bonus, a tree-laden with expensive gifts or someone to clean the house for the holidays.

If those are your desires, you are missing the heart of Christmas! If that is all that you can ask for, may I humbly submit to you that you have Christmas all wrong! You are missing the difficult yet sacred lesson that the life of Mary teaches all of us today:

Our plans pale in comparison to His interruptions! The most significant and meaningful desire that you will ever embrace is to ask God to interrupt your life with His love and His plans.

What these verses don't describe is the public outrage that Mary had yet to face. This girl, who has just had her world rocked with a message from heaven, would now be spat upon and cursed as she walked by. Formerly she was known as "pure" and a "virgin", and now her reputation was one of a loose and promiscuous woman. Perhaps now as Mary daily walked to the village well, she heard the coarse language of the men calling out nasty innuendos accompanied by raucous laughter.

Mary learned, as we all must, that Christmas is not about "self". Christmas calls all of us to die to self, to sacrifice preference and to forgo normalcy. Christmas is the clarion call that convinces a person never to live for only human purposes ever again. We have all been embraced by the call of Christmas that resounds from Mary's heart into our world today, "Live for His purposes! Live for Christ alone!"

Christmas is about the intervention of God into our ordinary lives; it is about Christ being born into our disappointments and failures.

Christmas is not about me but it is about Christ revealing Himself in me and to me! Now that's something to celebrate!

BIBLE READING

- Luke 1:36-38
- Genesis 18:1-4

LET THERE BE JOY IN ME

Do you truly believe that nothing is impossible with God?

_____

_____

_____

What is your one "impossible" prayer request this Christmas? Write it out and give it to God.

_____

_____

_____

DAY 8

The Resolve of Your Heart

Mary, the very young, but specifically chosen mother of Jesus, utters one of the most courageous statements in all of Scripture. In response to the announcement of the angel that Mary's world had just been interrupted with heaven's plan, Mary clearly and humbly declared, *"Behold the bondslave of the Lord, may it be done to me according to your word."* — (Luke 1:38)

A "bondslave" was a slave who was able to go free but instead chose to stay and serve his or her master. Mary willingly chose to offer temporary housing to the Savior of the world because that was God's desire. When her world collided with God's ultimate desire, Mary died to self and submitted to God the Father.

Has God asked something difficult of you? How have you responded? Have you said, *"Behold the bondslave of the Lord, may it be done to me according to Your word."*?

When God requires one of His children to lay down his or her way for His best plan, often there is a struggle of the human will. Unfortunately, rather than respond with the maturity and wisdom of the young Mary, many of us whine and complain. Some of us even may have the audacity to question whether or not God even knows what He is doing.

What has God asked of you? Has He asked you to love a difficult person? Perhaps He has asked you to raise a special needs child or to serve an uncaring boss. God is looking for bondslaves: He is in search of men and women who are willing to serve Him out of love. God is looking for those who willingly submit to His ways and plans simply because their heart completely belongs to Him. God desires men and women who will allow Him to interrupt their perfectly planned lives with His unbelievable and miraculous plans! Are you willing to be a bondslave of the Father?

Mary's pure heart and true resolve are revealed through the final words of her statement, *" ... May it be done to me according to your word."* Is that the resolve of your heart as well? When your will comes into conflict with God's Word, God's Word must win at all cost. Like Mary, settle this issue of human will and the authority of God's Word today. I declare, with Mary, that in my life, it will always be done according to His Word because I am His bondslave.

BIBLE READING

- Luke 1:38
- Psalm 119:1-16

LET THERE BE JOY IN ME

What is the hardest thing that God has ever asked of you? How have you responded?

_____

_____

_____

What does it mean to respond as a "bondslave"?

_____

_____

_____

What are some of the heart attitudes that a "bondslave" would embrace?

_____

_____

_____

DAY 9

Disappointment and Heartache

Engagement is one of the very happiest and dreamiest of times in the life of a young couple. It is the singular moment in life when all hours are spent imagining the incomparable joy that is to come with marriage. It is the extraordinary time in one's life when love seems perfect and trustworthy.

However, Mary was forced to speak words to Joseph that certainly damaged their perfect love story.

"Joseph, I am with child."

Joseph and Mary's love story had been horribly and unexplainably interrupted. Mary had become pregnant and Joseph knew that he was not the father. Joseph surely must have wondered if Mary had been violated although she was quietly insistent that the child in her womb had been placed there by the Holy Spirit.

I wonder if Mary told him this ravaging news with tears running down her beautiful and innocent cheeks.

Did Joseph wonder if Mary was delusional? How else was it possible to explain this catastrophic turn of events? What was once lovely was now tinged with ugly. What was once anticipated was now dreaded.

Joseph was a righteous man whose pure heart was breaking because his bride was with child and he knew that it was not his child. Mary, his lovely and sweet Mary, had surely been taken advantage of by someone. She was the kindest girl he had ever known but was the stress of the planning the wedding causing her to break under the pressure? What *could* he do? What *should* he do?

Joseph apparently did not believe Mary's story because the Bible recounts that his plan was to put her away privately. Joseph knew that this was the kindest and most loving choice for a young man found in the throes of betrayal. He could have allowed his intended to be stoned before the baby was born. Or, after giving birth, he could have allowed both Mary and the baby to be stoned. Sending his betrothed away and never to be heard from again was the ultimate loving sacrifice on Joseph's part.

It is impossible to even imagine Joseph's disappointment with God and with the person whom he had loved the most in the world. Mary had been the center of his world and now he would never see her again. Did Joseph believe that the girl of his dreams had given her virginity to another man?

Joseph did not deserve this betrayal or this heartbreak. What he "deserved" was a wedding day filled with joy and the promise of young love.

Now, perhaps, Joseph's reputation had been sullied on the streets of Nazareth and his boyhood friends were snickering behind his back.

Joseph had to face Mary's parents and his own parents. Although he bore no guilt there was still the possibility that they would not believe him. There was no nuptial frivolity for this disappointed, heartbroken young man. All hopes of love and joy and promise had been dashed with the announcement of an early pregnancy.

Are you encountering deep disappointment with others as you face Christmas this year?

My prayer is that you will allow the promise of Christmas to overshadow the painful realities of your life. Christmas should never be minimized or ignored due to the disappointing realities of life; human disappointment should always be overcome by the promise that Christmas only brings.

BIBLE READING

- Matthew 1:18 & 19
- Romans 5:1-5

LET THERE BE JOY IN ME

What is the most difficult disappointment that you have ever faced? Does Christmas help ease the pain of disappointment or does it exacerbate it?

_____

_____

_____

How does Romans 5:1-5 encourage you?

_____

_____

_____

Do Not Be Afraid

Joseph was a righteous man ... a good man ... and a kind man. The word "righteous" in Matthew 1:19 is defined this way in the Greek: *"used of him whose way of thinking, feeling and acting is wholly conformed to the will of God."*

Joseph was not making decisions based upon his own best interest but his decisions were birthed in the conviction of God's perfect and holy will. Joseph was learning a significant lesson this first Christmas season; Joseph was discovering that celebrating the Savior is not about maximizing your own desires or preferences but it is about doing whatever it takes to welcome the Christ Child into your life.

This is a sobering lesson that perhaps we all should grapple with this Christmas season. Christmas is not about how I feel, about my circumstances, or about the comfort of family and friends. Christmas has always been and will eternally continue to be about making room for Jesus in the disappointed hallways of life.

Joseph planned to send Mary away privately although he could have had her stoned in the village square. Joseph's wise and kind plans, born in the heart of his best intentions, were interrupted by a Christmas angel! How wonderful to know that even when we are doing what we believe to be the highest good, God's ways are still higher than our best intentions! Christmas is a time when heaven's best interrupts our good.

And what were the first words that came out of this angel's beatific mouth? *"Joseph, son of David, do not be afraid ..."*

The words spoken to Joseph over 2,000 years ago ring clearly across the ages into our disappointment. *"Do not be afraid,"* is the message of Christmas to your life today.

Has God interrupted your life lately? Perhaps this Christmas it would be wise to take stock of your life and realize that God has the authority to interrupt your mundane. God has the power of showing you a better way to navigate life's challenges. Your very best human decision and noblest of plans pale in comparison to what God has for you!

Was Joseph just an ordinary boy in love with an ordinary girl named Mary?! Not a chance! God always has plans other than ordinary for those who choose a lifestyle of uncompromising righteousness. God desires to use each one of us as the vehicle through which Christ is revealed to every generation.

If you think that Christmas was only about Joseph and Mary and that you have been left out of the Christmas equation, you are emphatically and sadly wrong. You might as well join the Grinch and Ebenezer Scrooge in your opinion of the miracle of Christmas.

God longs to birth Christmas *through* you at this time in history. You are here to reveal the character and the heart of God. This is what righteous people have always been called to do for the Kingdom of God. The calling of Christmas does not only happen for one day of a calendar year! The call of Christmas is a lifetime call to exhibit the presence of Jesus.

BIBLE READING

- Matthew 1:18-25
- Colossians 1:25-29

LET THERE BE JOY IN ME:

Pray this year that Jesus would interrupt your holiday plans. Ask Him to invade your ordinary life with His extraordinary.

_____

_____

_____

What fear issue does the presence of Jesus help you deal with?

_____

_____

_____

The John-Jump!

Elizabeth was basking in the miracle of a surprise pregnancy even though she was well passed the age of childbearing. When Elizabeth was in her sixth month, Mary, her much younger relative, arrived at her house. A heavenly messenger had just informed Mary that she had been chosen to carry the Savior of the world.

Mary "went in a hurry" to the home of Elizabeth, the wife of a priest who had also been raised in the home of a priest. Perhaps Mary was longing for the stability and peace found in the home of Elizabeth. Perhaps Mary was trying to escape the wagging tongues and the crude remarks made at the village well. Perhaps Mary's parents sent her to the older and wiser Elizabeth because they didn't know what else to do with the outrageous story that their formerly perfect young daughter had surely fabricated.

When Mary entered the home of Zacharias and Elizabeth, the baby boy within the womb of Elizabeth, jumped for joy! The instant that John, although unborn, sensed that he was in the presence of Jesus the Messiah, he began to leap for joy!

John, although still in his mother's womb and unable to see Jesus with his natural eyes, knew that he was in the presence of the Lord. There is only one possible response to the presence of the Lord and that is joy! Elizabeth expressed to Mary that this was no soft little nudging that she felt from the baby within but that it was a gargantuan leap! John was exploding with joy at being in the presence of Jesus!

"In His presence is fullness of joy!"

— Psalm 16:11

The spirit of John was responding to the Spirit of Jesus Christ where there is always fullness of joy.

Perhaps as the years went by, these cousins would play at one another's homes. I wonder if every time Jesus walked into the room if John, the lively one, would begin to jump up and down!

His mother, the proper Elizabeth, might have said, "John dear, stop jumping! You are being so lively, son."

"But mama, I just can't help it! Every time I am around Jesus my legs just start jumping for joy!" might have been this strong-willed son's response to the quiet and peaceful ways of his mother.

When Jesus walks into our world, into our lives and into our homes, we must respond with complete joy. Our heart should begin the John-jump!

In His presence is the only place that you will ever experience true and complete joy. Joy is not found in having your children home for Christmas, in giving and receiving mountains of gifts, in decorating the house like a picture in a magazine or in eating culinary concoctions that will satisfy your holiday taste buds. Those earthly delights are all connected to happiness but never to joy. Joy is found in one place and one place alone: *in His presence!*

Perhaps especially at Christmastime we are guilty of looking for joy in all the wrong places. This Christmas, make room for His presence. Spend time with your friends and family singing the beloved Carols of Christmas; read the story of His birth from the Bible with those you love. The greatest gift you will ever give to someone whom you love is the promise to pray for his or her heartfelt needs.

When Elizabeth told Mary that the baby within her womb "leaped for joy", the word used to describe this action is the Greek word "skirtao". The word "skirtao" is used only one other place in the New Testament.

> *"Blessed are you when men hate you, and ostracize you, and insult you, and scorn your name as evil, for the sake of the Son of Man. Be glad in that day and leap for (skirtao) for behold, your reward is great in heaven. For in the same way their fathers used to treat the prophets."*
>
> — Luke 6:22 & 23

The presence of Jesus will instigate a genuine leap for joy in an otherwise ordinary life. However, we are also expected to leap for joy when our life has fallen utterly and completely apart. When we have been vilified and rejected by people and when we have been victimized by unfair circumstances, that is the time that we are commanded by Jesus to skirtao!! To leap for joy!

There is no logical explanation for this joyful response in the face of emotional pain and deep disappointment but it is the healthiest response for a believer. You can jump! You can do the John-jump at the worst moment of your life because Jesus has promised never to leave you or forsake you.

This Christmas, respond to the joy of His presence especially if you are going through dark events and disappointing circumstances. May I just gently and sincerely tell you that there is really no earthly reason not to respond to Who Jesus is but with complete and utter joy? There is no circumstance, person or event that has the power to rob one of His children of the joy of His presence.

Christmas has given us the assurance that while living on earth, we can be the beneficiaries of heaven's joy! When Jesus came, He paved the way for joy!

Don't expect the festivities to relieve the pain – Only His presence can do that for you! When Jesus came to planet earth, He paved the way for heaven's joy to infiltrate our lives.

My prayer for you during this Christmas season is that you will know the joy of the presence of the Lord. I pray that like John you will respond to His presence in the most miraculous of ways. I pray that you will not mistakenly believe that joy is extracted from your circumstances but that you will worship the Baby in the manger and allow your heart to enter fully into the joy of Christmas.

BIBLE READING

- Luke 1:39-44

LET THERE BE JOY IN ME

What is it in our life that is prohibiting you from doing the "John-jump"?

_____

_____

_____

What are some ways that you can practice the presence of Jesus which is where there is fullness of joy?

_____

_____

_____

Christmas Begins With Thanksgiving

One of my favorite but benign addictions in life is "people watching"! Now, I enjoy people-watching year round, but the time that it is most fascinating to me is at Christmastime. When I am in the post office line, waiting to mail my packages and cards, I intently observe and often eavesdrop on holiday conversations and frustrations. When I find myself at the mall, while trying not to be impatient, what brings pleasure to me is to focus my attention on others who are frustratingly focused on the buying of gifts and on the possibility of seasonal sales. I often try to butt into conversations with words of encouragement or Christmas joy!

Would you like to join me in eavesdropping on one of

the most glorious Christmas conversations in all of history? I believe that this one celebratory exchange just may change your heart forever!

After the elder Elizabeth had blessed the Baby Boy in Mary's virgin womb, Mary began to worship the Lord. She broke out into a powerful response of worship and heartfelt adoration! I have often wondered if, when declaring these words of praise, she fell to her knees and lifted her hands toward heaven!

"My soul exalts the Lord!"

This simple, exclamatory sentence were the first words out of Mary's grateful mouth in Elizabeth's presence. Mary's choice of words becomes especially beautiful when one realizes that the "soul" is the birthplace of passions, emotions, aversions and desires. Mary's soul was not in a state of confusion or denial but Mary was declaring the fact that regardless of circumstances and events that her emotions and desires would always take her to a place of worship. Mary spent no time rehearsing what a difficult position God had placed her in or how embarrassed she was at what her family had to go through. Mary took her emotions and her feelings to a place of genuine praise and worship.

"And my spirit has rejoiced in God my Savior." Mary's soul and spirit were joining in a beautiful duet of thanksgiving. One's spirit is the place in the human constitution that desires the Lord and all that He has. The spirit is the place of walking by faith and not by sight. In this spirit place of Mary's life that was in constant communion with the Spirit of God, her response was identical to that of her soul: sincere and eruptive rejoicing!

How are you responding to circumstances or events that you don't understand or perhaps might not choose? What is your soul spending time doing this Christmas season? Is your soul out of control with spending, eating and impatience? Or has your soul observed the example of Mary and chosen to exalt the Lord?

My prayer is that your spirit and your soul will fall to their knees and that you will lift your hands and your voice toward heaven! I pray that eavesdropping on this one holiday conversation will change the choices that you make not only at Christmastime but in every day of the coming year.

BIBLE READING

- Luke 1:46-56

LET THERE BE JOY IN ME

Why is it so hard to rejoice in the Lord when our circumstances
are difficult?

_____

_____

_____

Make a list of 5-10 Scriptures that you can quote during difficult
days of life.

_____

_____

_____

_____

_____

_____

_____

_____

_____

_____

_____

_____

_____

_____

DAY 13

God is Always On Time

Elizabeth was too old to have a baby by human standards. Her body had long ceased to exhibit the possibility of reproduction. Elizabeth had been unable to conceive and bear a child even when she was young and in her childbearing years. Now, as a woman who had lived nearly 9 decades of life, there was no human possibility that becoming pregnant would ever happen to the righteous and faithful Elizabeth. There was not a sliver of hope that Elizabeth would ever hold a biological newborn baby in her wrinkled arms!

But our God breaks all of the constraints of human standards. His ways are higher than our ways and He is able to trump any limitation that we exhibit even in our strength.

"Now the time had come for Elizabeth to give birth ..."

Certainly this "time" was not Elizabeth's chosen time. God has a chosen time for prayers to be answered, for His mission to be accomplished and for miracles to take place. Elizabeth's chosen "time" had most certainly been when she was a young woman but God's chosen time involved a miracle! Do not mistakenly believe that God has forgotten you or that He has not heard your prayers. When God's appointed time comes in its fullness, you will give birth to all that God has planned for you.

"Her neighbors and her relatives heard that the Lord had displayed His great mercy toward her; and they were rejoicing with her."

Many times I believe that the Lord says "Wait" as an answer to our desperate prayers so that His glory is revealed rather than the certainty of mankind's function. Most women are able to conceive and bear children in their teens and twenties and even into their thirties and early forties, but it takes the intervention of God for a woman to experience the miracle of birth when in her eighth decade of life!

Can you imagine the rejoicing of her relatives and neighbors? Can you picture the scene as the women danced in circles in the village streets? Can you envision how her friends lifted their hands in praise to Yahweh?

As John nestled into his mother's arms, and as the nearly 100 year-old eyes of Zacharias looked into the newborn eyes of his son, God was glorified. Prayers had been answered. Their story had just begun.

The story of Elizabeth and Zacharias is the call to live a righteous life and it is the promise of what persevering prayer will certainly obtain. God is more than able to accomplish all that concerns you. His part is to perform the miracles ... your part is to pray without ceasing and to live a life that pleases His heart.

BIBLE READING

- Luke 1:57-80
- Psalm 138

LET THERE BE JOY IN ME

What has been the greatest miracle or answer to pray that you have ever experienced? Write it out and share it with your family this Christmas season.

_____

_____

_____

_____

_____

_____

_____

_____

_____

_____

Define the word "miracle".

_____

_____

_____

_____

_____

DAY 14

The "Busy" of Bethlehem

After Mary returned home from visiting Elizabeth, it seems that Joseph and Mary had a private and hurried wedding ceremony. There would be no grand wedding feast or public vows. Everything had changed for this young, chosen couple. They had to travel to Bethlehem, many miles from their hometown, to register for a census.

Bible historians believe that there may have been as many as 1 million visitors slogging the streets of this small, ancient city named "Bethlehem".

What would happen if one million people invaded your town? What would that do to the traffic patterns? What would one million extra holiday visitors do to the lines at your already crowded mall? Would the hotels in your hometown be able to accommodate that many out of town guests? Do you think that there would be any possible way to get a reservation at your favorite restaurant with one million extra people converging in your city?

When Mary and Joseph arrived in Bethlehem for the census, I am sure that it was probably much like any mall on the day after Thanksgiving in every city in western civilization. There was no MapQuest to find your way or priceline.com to pre-book a hotel room.

We have never experienced "busy" compared to Bethlehem on this momentous night. There were donkeys braying and vendors shouting; there was a cavalcade of camels, people, tax collectors and city officials pushing and shoving their way through the dusty streets of Bethlehem. There was the odor of manure and the smell of crushed and sweating bodies on every corner of every street.

People's nerves were taut, their pocketbooks were empty and they were all fed up with a greedy government! It was a mass of humanity who didn't know where they were or how to get to where they needed to go. Sounds a lot like the 21st. Century, doesn't it?!

God chose this moment of chaos and confusion ... of frayed nerves and economic failure ... as the birthplace of His Son. God chose to invade the traffic jams of humanity with His little Boy.

We have allowed our lives to become as chaotic, confusing and out of control as any city, in any part of the world, at any time in history. The beauty of Christmas is that it was His presence that changed the purpose of the busy-ness!

God desired to neutralize our expensive way of living and so He sent the Prince of Peace.

God knew that we would need an answer for our stress-induced meltdowns and so He sent heaven's Darling to be our answer.

In the midst of the mess of humanity and into the endless voices of questions with no answers, a Savior was born. My prayer is that this year, in the middle of your overly active life, you will have time to gaze in wonder at the Baby in the manger.

Do not be so wrapped up in the temporary aspects of the season that you miss the divine appointments of Christmas and the glory of it all! The glory of Christmas has always been and will always be the miracle of His presence ... a newborn baby lying in a manger.

BIBLE READING

- Luke 2:1-6
- Isaiah 26:3&4

LET THERE BE JOY IN ME

Make a list of all of the things that keep you "too busy" during the Christmas season. How can you shorten this list?

_____

_____

_____

_____

_____

_____

_____

_____

Plan a family night, or a gathering of friends, when you simply enjoy the Savior. Plan to read the Christmas story from the Bible and sing some well-loved Christmas Carols. Pray for one another.

DAY 15

The Wonder of a Baby

It probably took Mary and Joseph nearly a week to travel the 80 miles from Nazareth to Bethlehem due to Mary's advanced pregnancy. Although the timing of the journey was inconvenient, perhaps it was a relief to get away from the wagging tongues at the village well and the old women who were counting the months on their fingers. Mary and Joseph were required to travel away from their hometown in order to register for the census that had been decreed by Caesar Augustus.

As Mary and Joseph entered Bethlehem, the streets were teeming with a mass of humanity. It was in those moments, while Mary was being jostled by the crowds, that she felt the first of her labor pains. Perhaps her water broke on the crowded street, wetting her garment and the donkey on which she was riding.

Did she quietly whisper while in pain, "Joseph! Please find a place for me to rest!"

Joseph found nothing more than a cave ... a barn ... a stable in which to prepare for the quickly approaching arrival of their Son.

The smelly stable was rife with manure and unkempt animals; the hard ground was saturated with the urine of the barnyard creatures and the clean hay was sparse. Cobwebs were drooping from the ceiling while a mouse or two scurried by in fear. The cows were munching on the pungent hay and sheep were sadly looking on as Mary labored and bled. It was into this putrid atmosphere of mankind that the Savior entered the world!

My heart stops as I picture the enchanted face of this teen-age mother meeting her baby Boy for the very first time! She was gazing into the face of God ... and He was looking back at her. God had wrapped his tiny hand around her finger and around her heart as well.

He was her Son ... yet her Lord. He was her Baby ... yet her Majesty.

Mary was spellbound not only by the ten tiny fingers and the ten miniature toes, but she was spellbound by the presence of God. Who did this little person look like? Did he have Mary's father's nose? Or did He display Joseph's father's ears? What we do know is that He came equipped with the heart of God.

Mary could not take her eyes off of her baby Boy so great was her love for this heaven-sent Child. And the most amazing miracle of all was that He could not take His eyes off of his young mother, a specimen of the world that He came to save, so great was His love for mankind.

Don't take your eyes off of the true meaning of Christmas. Know that when Jesus was born ... He was born for you. Allow the Baby in the manger to wrap His love around your heart.

BIBLE READING

- Luke 2:1-7
- John 1:1-18

LET THERE BE JOY IN ME

Make a list of the reasons why you believe that God sent His Son
Jesus to the world.

_____

_____

_____

_____

_____

_____

_____

As you ponder these reasons, now make a list of appropriate
ways in the 21st. Century to celebrate the grand entrance of Jesus
unto planet earth.

_____

_____

_____

_____

_____

_____

_____

DAY 16

They are Playing Your Song

Shepherds were dirty, uneducated men with grime under their fingernails and sludge in their brains. There were a group of these shepherds one night, huddled around a fire in the inky, black of night. These muddy specimens of humanity were cold and shivering while trying to stay awake. Their only responsibility in life was to keep track of a herd of dumb sheep that were restless, disobedient and lice-infested.

Shepherds were a hopeless crew of men with nothing to look forward to because they knew that nothing about their lives would ever change. Life can become quickly pointless if you are a man who lives with sheep drool on his clothes and sheep dung between his toes.

This night ... this particular night ... was no different from thousands of other dark, cold lonely nights for this woebegone band of brothers. When the night couldn't get any blacker and the sheep couldn't get any more cantankerous, suddenly, in an instant of time, something so miraculous happened that life would never again be the same for these men. And the miracle of it all is that life will never be the same for you or for me as well.

Unexpectedly, heaven exploded into their small, cold and dark world. The song of the angels burst forth into the war zone of earth and proclaimed the joy of heaven into the hopeless and meaningless existence of the shepherds. Stars were falling and bursting in rare and glorious colors while the heavens opened and a majestic angel choir began to sing a mighty symphony that can still be heard today!

Jesus invaded this dark, cold world with heaven's joy and it is still His gift to you today. His presence in your life makes shepherds dance and angels sing. Your heart can become an explosion of joy because of the birth of a Baby over 2,000 years ago.

You can receive joy because of Jesus ... you can walk in peace because of this Baby.

"And behold, we bring you good news of great joy which shall be to all the people; for unto you is born this day in the City of David a Savior who is Christ the Lord."

—Luke 2:10

The first word that the angels used to describe the birth of Jesus Christ was the word "joy" and I believe that it should be the first word used to describe you as well! Joy is the birthmark of a Christian because when you accept Jesus into your heart you are branded for life with His joy. You have become a vessel of His presence where there is always fullness of joy.

Your life has now become purposeful as you carry the Christ child to this inky, restless world. The hopelessness of your life has dissipated because you now understand the honor of transmitting the joy of His presence to the muddy specimens of humanity.

The song of the angels was never meant to be heard only by a solitary group of shepherds. When the angels sang that night, they were singing to those of you with the drool of life upon your heart and the dung of circumstances in your soul. The symphony of heaven ricochets through the ages and has as its focused destination your cold and lonely existence. Joy truly has come to your world and nothing will ever be the same again!

BIBLE READING

- Luke 2:8-11

LET THERE BE JOY IN ME

Plan an evening of singing Christmas Carols this season. Perhaps you could invite some friends to your home to sing or even go to a nursing home or hospital to sing the great lyrics of the season.

_____

_____

_____

As you sing, let the meaning of the lyrics cleanse the drool and the dung of life that has fallen upon you.

_____

_____

_____

DAY 17

The Song of the Angels

David Taylor came home sad and discouraged from school one day in early November. With tears rolling down his freckled cheeks, he told his mother that his teacher told him that he couldn't sing in the Christmas program.

"She said that I am awful and that I sing too loud," David explained between sobs.

David's father was sitting in the living room reading the afternoon's paper and overheard his son's heartbreak. Mr. Taylor was indignant and furious. How could any teacher do this to any child?

Mr. Taylor decided to help his son learn how to sing and after dinner that night, he took David into the living room and had him stand beside the family piano. Mr. Taylor began to play the familiar melody of "It Came Upon a Midnight Clear". As David opened his mouth, a cat-like screech came out.

"David, part of singing is listening. Listen ... then sing," instructed the patient father. *"It came upon a midnight clear, that glorious song of old."*

David's second attempt was worse than his first! But when the father was tempted to give up, he thought of the unfeeling teacher and realized, "If a father doesn't do this, who will?"

And so they continued, a patient father and his little boy, night after November night. *"... From angels bending near the earth to touch their harps of gold."*

The days of November faded into December, while Mr. Taylor and David spent every evening at the piano going over and over and over the melody to the song. *"Peace on the earth good will to men from heaven's all gracious King. "*

And finally, the night before David was scheduled to sing before his teacher, the entire Taylor family gathered around the piano and declared, *"The world in solemn stillness lay, to hear the angels sing."* There was a satisfied silence at the end of the final stanza as the family grinned at each other. David had learned! David could sing!

When the day came that David sang for his teacher, she said that he could be in the program! David was front and center in the third-grade Christmas concert. He was angelic and on pitch as the song ended with the glorious thought,

> *"For lo, the days are hastening on, by prophet seen of old,*
> *When with the ever circling years shall come the time foretold;*
> *When peace shall over all the earth, its ancient splendors fling,*
> *And the whole world send back the song which now the*
>   *angels sing!"*

Learning to sing had somehow changed the little boy, David Taylor. While other children were making Christmas lists for Santa and stealing frosted cookies from the jar, David was by the piano, plunking out simple Christmas melodies. When his siblings were out sledding and skating, David was singing at the piano, *"Hark! The herald angels sing, 'Glory to the newborn King!"* Once the song of Christmas had nestled in David's heart and voice, it had captured every ounce of his being.

On Christmas Eve, after the family had hung their stockings with care and left out the requisite cookies for the jolly old man of myth, Mr. Taylor looked out the window and saw his pajama-clad boy in the front yard looking toward the sky.

The father quietly walked out the front door and put his arms around David without saying a word. The son leaned into his father's chest and said, "The world is lying still, Dad. Just like the song says."

"Do you hear them, Dad? Do you hear the angel's singing? I hear them ... do you, Dad?"

The father thought that he was teaching a little boy to sing a sweet song at Christmas time but what had really happened was that the little boy had taught them both to listen ... to listen for the angel's song.

BIBLE READING

- Luke 1: 13 & 14
- Psalm 148

LET THERE BE JOY IN ME

What is your favorite childhood Christmas memory? Perhaps you could write it out and share it with your family this Christmas.

_____

_____

_____

_____

_____

_____

_____

_____

_____

_____

_____

Go to a school or a church Christmas concert this year and enjoy the faces of the children.

DAY 18

Do Not Be Afraid!

Angels are an intrinsic and dynamic part of the Christmas story. Christmas simply would not have happened without these God-sent messengers from heaven. We don't know whether or not the angels were clothed in flowing, white robes, whether they had a halo that was sparkling or even whether or not they flew with wings into the Christmas scene, but what we do know is that these angels carried the heart of God concerning the momentous event that was about to take place!

Angels appear four times in the traditional Christmas story and each time, although they carried different pieces of information concerning what was to happen, their message is always the same, *"Do not be afraid!"* It was what the angel said first to Zachariah, then to Mary, then to Joseph and finally to the shepherds on the hillside.

"Do not be afraid!"

I believe that this just may be the message that heaven is sending to your heart this Christmas season. Christmas exuberantly declares that Jesus and fear are mutually exclusive. When Jesus arrives on the scene, there is no reason to be afraid. His presence powerfully removes any reason for fear.

It is time for you to step away from your fear and boldly walk into His presence. I pray that this Christmas, and for every day of the coming year, that you will realize that when Jesus has been birthed in your heart, there is absolutely no reason for fear or for worry. The message of Christmas has not changed much in 2,000 years and I can guarantee that the words of the angels are still ringing clearly into our 21st. Century world, *"Do not be afraid!"*

When your circumstances are falling apart, remind yourself, *"Do not be afraid!"*

When there is not enough money to pay the bills, remind yourself, *"Do not be afraid!"*

When you are dealing with disappointment, pain or loneliness, remind yourself, *"Do not be afraid!"*

Jesus has been identified as the "Prince of Peace" by Isaiah who prophesied the coming of the Messiah. Jesus, the Son of God, has been given ruling authority in the realm of peace. And, in reality, you will never experience true and abiding peace without first experiencing His presence in your life. You will never be the beneficiary of the sweetness of peace without first allowing Jesus to rule and reign in you.

God has promised that He would give His peace to those whose hearts and minds are fully stayed on Him. Peace is not the absence of trouble but it is the very real presence of God. And because of Jesus, this Christmas, and every Christmas, you can rest in His overwhelming and satisfying peace!

BIBLE READING

- Matthew 1:20
- Luke 1:30
- Luke 1:13
- Luke 2:10

LET THERE BE JOY IN ME

What are some of the issues that cause fear to creep into your heart? Today, apply Isaiah 26:3 to those issues.

_____

_____

_____

_____

_____

_____

_____

_____

_____

_____

_____

_____

DAY 19

Academic Weirdos!

The Magi specialized in astronomy, which is the study of the stars. These learned, cerebral men were not Jews but were pagan astrologers from the East. Today we might call these wise men "diviners" or "magicians". They were certainly wise in the way of secular science. The Magi are probably the types of people that you and I would stay away from today. Perhaps, in the 21st. Century, we would label them as "humanists" or on "the left side of academia", while internally we might be calling them "weirdos". Quite frankly … these wealthy, esteemed men were little more than academic nuts!

These magic men came to King Herod asking where they could find the new king; it was their ultimate plan to worship and revere Him Who was born King of the Jews.

King Herod was perturbed at this news and gathered the scribes and priests to figure out where the Messiah was to be born. These leading church scholars of the day were able to quote to King Herod a prophetic word from Micah that confirmed that the heaven sent Ruler would be born in Bethlehem.

King Herod then called for a second meeting with the Magi and sent them to Bethlehem, telling them to let him know when the Messiah was found because, he proclaimed that he, too, desired to come and worship this new born King.

Now the question that should be asked at this juncture in this historical account is this one, "Was King Herod actually going to worship Jesus?" And the answer is an emphatic, "Absolutely not!"

King Herod was plotting to kill the Baby who had come to bring peace on earth! The worship that King Herod intended was mere lip service. His heart had no intent of worshipping the Christ Child although his mouth construed a thoughtless and irreverent lie with the desire of manipulating the plans of the Magi.

What is your plan this Christmas? Will you only give him your lip service? Will you say that He is Lord while acting in quite a different manner? Christmas is a time when the motives of our hearts are laid bare.

Will you worship Him with only your mouth ... or will your heart and your life join in the high praise that He deserves? Only you can determine this type of worship.

You choose whether to worship Him with lip service alone or bring to Jesus, the Baby in the manger, the worship that is accompanied by a lifetime of loving actions.

BIBLE READING

- Matthew 2:1-8

LET THERE BE JOY IN ME

Do you have anyone in your life who does not believe in Jesus? What gift could you give to them this year that demonstrates your true love for them?

_____

_____

_____

What does it mean to worship the King? Does worship always involve singing? If not, what are some other ways that you can worship the Christ Child this Christmas season?

_____

_____

_____

_____

_____

_____

_____

_____

_____

_____

_____

_____

DAY 20

Violent Joy!

The star led the Magi to the Light of the World! The wise men did not need the advice or navigation powers of King Herod and his best men - they just needed to follow the Light of the World.

Whom or what have you been following this Christmas Season? Are you so tightly bound to the whims of the culture that all you can think about are sales, calories, postal lines and parties? If you use those temporary signposts as the compass that guides you toward all things Christmas, you are going to be quickly lost in the swamp of holiday fluff. However, if you can fix your heart and your gaze on the Star of Bethlehem then you will assuredly be led to a time of wonderment and worship.

When the magnificent star stopped the Magi in their wealthy tracks, the Bible says that these learned men, "rejoiced exceedingly with great joy". And what a celebration began that night!

Only 6 words: "rejoiced exceedingly with great joy" yet what richness their brevity holds. These 6 simple words are some of the most expressive words in all of Scripture.

"Rejoiced" is translated as "let the hope of future blessedness give you joy! What rich intent and calling! This word communicates to all of us, from every generation and at every moment in all of recorded history, that because of the Baby born in the manger, we can look ahead not with dread and worry but with hope and expectation. When you encounter Jesus, there is reason to rejoice because of the many blessings headed in your direction.

"Exceedingly" is defined as "greatly" or even "violently" or vehemently.

These first century professorial types did not just quietly bow down with their scholarly hands clasped in front of their wise faces. The joy that they experienced in the presence of Jesus was an explosion of joy that knocked their mortarboards off their wizened heads!

The joy of Jesus rocked their academic world! These men were jumping up and down in the presence of the Baby Boy King. These brilliant men were participating in the John-jump!

The Magi were whooping and hollering because after years of study, after decades of hitting dead-ends as to the meaning of life, after a lifetime of frustrating nothingness, they had found the Creator of this miraculous universe. They had at long last discovered the Answer to all of their unanswerable questions and they had now been able to discern the wisdom of the Ages in a toddler's sweet babble.

These erudite men were participating in a violent explosion of joy! The joy that Jesus delivers into your life should shake some things up a bit!

What needs shaking up in your life this season as a response to all that He is? The Magi had at last found a reason to celebrate because they had found the source of eternal joy.

"Great" in this sentence means "with great effort of the affections and emotions of the mind". It is significant that this particular definition of the word "great" includes the word for "mind". The Magi were men of scrolls and cerebral intensity; at the moment this star stopped in the presence of Jesus, all that they had ever learned or studied paled in comparison to this one momentous event.

Being in the presence of the Creator of the Universe was such a life-changing opportunity that it infiltrated the very way that they thought and processed information.

And finally, but far from least in meaning, the word "joy" is rich in depth and in texture because it is defined as "the blessedness that the Lord enjoys". When these pedantic men discovered the location of the Baby Boy, they also tapped into the mother lode of joy! They hit a vein so rich and generous in joy that it changed every detail, both large and small, concerning their impressive lives.

Every blessing that the Lord has ... the Magi had ... and you now have ... because of Christmas!

BIBLE READING

- Matthew 2:9 & 10

LET THERE BE JOY IN ME

Does joy have anything to do with our circumstances at all?

_____

_____

_____

What has been the most joyful moment of your life?

_____

_____

_____

A Change in Position and in Prominence

The Magi fell on their faces and worshiped Jesus. This was full-blown, dynamic heart worship and not mere lip service in the manner of King Herod. King Herod "said" that he wanted to worship the King of the Jews but it was lip service alone that was his intention. While King Herod spoke of worship, it was murder that was in his ugly heart.

These learned and respected men, the Magi, who had possibly traveled as far as 800 or 900 miles to find the new born King, fell on their faces when in His dear presence. Jesus was a baby, probably under 2 years old, when they arrived and yet still they fell down in wonder and in worship. While Jesus was talking baby talk and babbling in a language only his mother could understand, these men who were known for solving the mysteries of the ages, lay prostrate in His eternal presence.

True worship always entails a change of position and a change in prominence. In the presence of the Holy Child, these men cared not for tradition or liturgy. They only knew that this little bit of a Boy was worthy to be worshiped and so they fell at His baby feet in heartfelt praise.

Will you fall on your face this Christmas in the presence of Jesus? True worship always involves joy! These wise men had their academic world rocked with the joy that was found in the presence of Jesus Christ. They had changed their academic regalia for a garment of praise.

Will you let go of your very human, emotional make-up and allow the joy of His presence to infiltrate all of the corners of your world?

True worship always involves a giving away of something valuable. The Magi had brought treasures to the tiny King and His humble family. What will you bring of value to Jesus this Christmas? The Magi gave gifts fit for a King and what we offer Him can be no less.

Worship is the meeting place of God and humanity. It is the moment when humanity falls on its face in joy!

The mistake that many of us make is that we are distracted by the "magic" of the season when what is actually occurring is the miraculous. The miracle of Christmas is just one choice away. Will you mistakenly yearn for snow, gifts and family? Or will you lift your eyes to the miracle of Christmas?

You are loved so much … that a miracle has happened! It is a miracle that divinity would be joined with our humanity! It is a bona fide miracle that heaven would sing into our souls! It is a miracle of heavenly proportions that where there was once confusion and conflict and sin … now there is joy and peace!

BIBLE READING

- Matthew 2:11

LET THERE BE JOY IN ME

What item of value can you give to Jesus this year? Is it your time? Is it a heartfelt gift to someone who is in need? Is it the gift of encouragement?

_____

_____

_____

Make a list of three people who need your friendship this year and then make arrangements to spend time with them over the holiday season

_____

_____

_____

_____

_____

_____

_____

_____

_____

_____

The Star in You

"*And having been warned by God in a dream not to return to Herod, the magi left for their own country.*"

—Matthew 2:12

When a man or a woman engages in wholehearted worship and gives something of value to the King of Kings, how easy it then becomes to hear the voice of God! Prior to this incredible event, the Magi depended on earthly directions and upon man's best judgment. Now, because they knew Jesus, because they had fallen on their faces in His presence and because they had given to Him that which was of value, the guidance of God was easy to discern.

Worship, in a believer's life, always turns up the volume of heaven! The Magi were accustomed to obtaining all of their knowledge from the patterns of the stars, from scrolls of the great minds of historical prominence and from earthly governments. Now these men heard the voice of the God of the ages! These men are discovering the wisdom of obtaining their directions from God and from God alone.

Not only did they hear His voice but they also obeyed His voice! This was quite a change for men who formerly had so esteemed academic prestige!

God warned the wise men in a dream to return home on a different route from the way on which they had come. Herod intended to kill the newborn King of the Jews and was waiting to procure His location from the Magi if they returned through Jerusalem.

Worship not only enables a human being to hear the voice of God but worship often changes one's direction in life as well. Worship will give a new perspective on destiny and will determine the road that you should take in order to arrive at God's intended location for your life. Never underestimate the role that both worship and sincere giving play in enabling you to reach your ultimate destiny in Christ.

Just like the Magi, God may want you to hear and consider His voice alone and thereby change your direction. Your part in life's equation is to worship Him completely and to give to Him sacrificially. Worship and giving from the heart have always been, and will always continue to be, the most important parts of Christmas.

The wise men represent our culture and its misconstrued value of commercialism, humanism and materialism. The wise men also represent humanity on a quest and on a journey for true meaning in life.

I believe that when Christians begin to celebrate Christmas with sincere worship and in generous giving that our culture, however currently misguided, will begin to see the Star in us. I also believe that when we are brave enough to celebrate Christmas with joy and with peace … with gladness and rejoicing … with love and purpose … that commercialism will pale in comparison

God cares about how you celebrate Christmas ... He actually cares very much about the choices that you are making this achingly beautiful and most sacred season of the year. God cares because Christmas is the greatest gift that He has ever given to those whom He loved the very most!

BIBLE READING

- Matthew 2:12

LET THERE BE JOY IN ME;

What are some of the traditional ways of celebrating Christmas that you can let minimize in order to celebrate it in a more genuine and worshipful manner?

_____

_____

_____

_____

_____

_____

Give the gift of prayer to someone this year. Commit to pray for someone who is discouraged every day of the coming year.

_____

_____

_____

DAY 23

Gifts Galore!

Did you know that Christmas is all about presents?! Now ... before the self-righteous Scrooge of your personality rears it's miserly head ... let's think about it for a minute.

Every joy-filled day of this miraculous season ... every holiday cookie that is lovingly baked ... every Christmas card that is hurriedly mailed is all about giving a gift. Every Christmas party that you attend is about giving the gift of your presence to a group of people. Every Christmas concert that you attend is about the gift of music being given to those in attendance. Every meal that you bake is about giving your time and love to the people in your home.

The intent of the heart of Christmas should be to give a gift to someone who has been an important and vital part of your life during the preceding year. Sometimes the gift is a loving sacrifice ... and at other times it is a necessary nuisance.

For some people you buy a gift because they feel that it is expected. For others, you may buy a gift because you, quite simply, wouldn't have it any other way. Many people buy gifts out of tradition or out of family demands but most gifts are bought and given out of heart-felt love. We give because we care and especially at Christmastime we long to express a small piece of our heart.

Heaven gave to every person in every generation the greatest Gift of all. The Bible says, "A Child has been born for us!" Imagine the miracle of that gift ... just drink in the joy that God gave the gift of His Son for you!

No matter how much I love a person ... no matter what value they have in my life ... no matter how they have served me during the preceding year ... I would never give away one of my children! But God the Father, loved you so much, that He gave His dearly loved and treasured Son to you one Christmas morning. You are the reason that God gave His Son.

The first Christmas, over 2000 years ago was all about presents! It was about a Gift that came from heaven with your name on it ... with love, from God! It wasn't wrapped in expensive red paper and tied with a bow of gold but it was a gift chosen especially for you just the same.

It was a present that Someone knew you were unable to live without. He knew that any good thing in your life would be because of this precious Gift. He intended that this particular Gift would change your life forever.

The gift has been given! The gift that has changed everything for you is a Baby in a manger. The Bible says, "God so loved the world that He gave His Son ... His only Son!" When you love somebody ... you just have to give to them! God loved you enough to give you what you wanted most of all: unconditional love and a never-ending song in your heart.

Will you receive heaven's gift this year? The gift has already been given and is yours to receive. It is the gift of a Father to His child. It is a gift that will guarantee heaven's entrance into all of your circumstances and it is a gift that will ensure your entrance into the joy of heaven.

BIBLE READING

- John 3:15-17
- I John 1:1-7

LET THERE BE JOY IN ME

What is the most precious gift that you have ever given to someone?

_____

_____

_____

Other than Christ, what is the most meaningful gift that you have ever received?

_____

_____

_____

Write a thank you note to one person this Christmas season for the gift that their life is to you.

_____

_____

The Gift of Joy!

Christmas has given to all of mankind the possibility of experiencing heaven's joy while living on earth. When Jesus came to earth, He paved the way for joy to come straight into your heart!

One of the most important aspects of Christmas is to respond to the joy of His presence. This is especially important if you are experiencing a circumstantial challenge or a gut-wrenching disappointment. Don't expect the festivities to relieve the pain - only His presence has the power to do that for you!

Nearly 800 years before the birth of Jesus, the Prophet Isaiah described exactly what the Messiah would do when He came:

"Surely our griefs He Himself bore and our sorrows He carried."

—Isaiah 53:4

Not only did Jesus come to take your sins to the cross, but He also came to relieve you of everything in life that has caused you to endure sorrow and to spend years of your life in deep grief. Jesus took your emotions of sorrow and grief and He carried them to the cross and died for them so that you could live with joy! God the Father knew that there would be events and circumstances this side of heaven that would cause deep pain and wretched grief in the hearts of His children. God, in His great mercy and lovingkindness was unwilling to allow you to bear the brunt of devastating emotions and disappointment. And so, as the greatest Christmas gift of all time, He said to Jesus, "Son, when You go to earth, not only will You take all of their sins to the cross, but You will also carry their sorrows and grief to the cross."

Christ took our sins to the cross so that we would no longer have to carry them or be in bondage to them. Christ took our sins so that our futures would not be determined by the sin in our lives. He took your grief and your sorrow for the same purpose. Jesus carried your emotional pain to the cross of Calvary so that you would no longer have to carry that pain. He took your mourning from you so that you would no longer be held captive by it. He removed your deepest emotional pain so that it no longer had the power to determine your future.

When Jesus came, the calendar page of history was turned and joy, in its fullest, was delivered to earth. Joy was given to you. When Jesus came from heaven's glory, He came to declare to your world, "Let there be joy!"

BIBLE READING

- Luke 6:17-23
- Isaiah 53:3-5
- Luke 1:44 & 45

LET THERE BE JOY IN ME

What is the one event or circumstance that has brought emotional pain and grief to your life this year? Can you give it to Jesus? Pray this prayer:

"Jesus, I give to You my emotional pain and sadness. I give to You my grief and my sorrow. I relinquish it to You. It's Yours forever … I never want it back again! And today, Jesus, I receive the joy of Your presence! Thank You that when You came to earth that You declared," Let There Be Joy!"

Let There Be Joy!

You may have heard the Christmas story a thousand times, but do you believe it? Have you embraced it as reality and truth? Or have you filed it away under Christmas fantasy along with magical bags of toys and elves? Is Christmas merely as significant to you as snowmen who dance, reindeer who sing and the false promise that all of your Christmases will be white?

The true Christmas story, the one that I have chosen to weave as truth into the fabric of my life is the story of a girl who was ordinary, young and unqualified. God chose to place Himself inside her womb so that you and I could, one day, carry His presence inside of our lives as well.

God, the Father, the Creator of the Universe, the Instigator of everything glorious and miraculous, chose you and I as the vehicle through which our generation would receive its greatest gift. It is our miracle that we have been called to demonstrate Jesus to the world in which we live.

The world will only experience the joy of His birth to the extent that I set aside my grief and pain and then embrace and exhibit His joy. The world will only taste the peace of His coming to the extent that I reveal the authority of His peace. The world will only know the hope of Christmas when I respond to pain and disappointment as an expectant believer. The world will only see the Light of the world when I allow my life to become a shining beacon to humanity. The world will only hear the song of Christmas when I sing it to the frozen, dark world of my culture.

Christmas was not all about Mary ... or Joseph ... or Elizabeth and Zacharias ... or the shepherds and the Magi. Christmas, in reality, is all about you! It is about you, making yourself available at this time in history to reveal the presence and love of our Savior. You are the joyful gift that today God is choosing to give to your world. Your generation is desperate to know the glory of a Savior. Without you, they may never know His name or the purpose of His coming.

As you now contemplate New Year's resolutions and plans that will encompass the 365 days to come, will you recommit yourself to be used by God? Will you decide this Christmas day to allow God to use your life as the manger upon which the Savior of the world may be found?

Will you allow the Father to use your life as the womb into which Jesus is delivered to the world? God has planted a seed of Himself in you. Will you respond like Mary with the submissive yet expectant words, *"Behold the bondslave of the Lord, be it unto me according to Your Word,"*?

Let there be joy! Jesus has been born in you. God is looking for believers who will be bold enough and joyful enough to embrace the miracle of Christmas not just one day a year but every day of every season.

BIBLE READING

- Isaiah 9:2-7
- Luke 2:1-20

LET THERE BE JOY IN ME

Now, after reading this devotional, define the word "Christmas". How has your definition changed after reading this devotional?

_____

_____

_____

As you make your New Year's Resolutions this year, resolve to be a receptacle of joy to a dark world. Make a list of 10 people who need your prayers, your faith and your joy. Resolve to pray for those 10 people every day and to bring Jesus into their lives.

_____

_____

_____

_____

_____

_____

_____

_____

_____

_____

_____

A Christmas Prayer

If you have never prayed this prayer, I'd like to invite you to pray it this year and to receive the greatest Christmas gift of all time:

"Jesus, I recognize you as the Savior of the world. Father God, thank You for sending Jesus into my dark and cold world. I am a sinner in need of a Savior. Jesus, will you forgive me of my sins and come into my heart today? Thank You for living in me and for one day taking me to heaven to live with You for all of eternity! In Jesus' Name, Amen."